TABLE OF CONTENTS

THE FOOD CHAIN

UNDER THE SEA

Lynn M. Stone

Rourke Publishing LLC
Vero Beach, Florida 32964

www.rourkepublishing.com

PHOTO CREDITS:
All photographs ©Marty Snyderman except pgs 4, 18 ©Lynn M. Stone

EDITORIAL SERVICES:
Pamela Schroeder

Library of Congress Cataloging-in-Publication Data

Stone, Lynn M.
    The food chain / Lynn M. Stone
        p. cm. — (Under the sea)
Includes bibliographical references (p.).
ISBN 1-58952-113-7
1. Marine ecology—Juvenile literature. 2. Food chains (Ecology)—
Juvenile literature. [1. Marine ecology. 2. Food chains (Ecology.] I. Title.

QH541.5.S3 S69 2001
577.7'16—dc21   2001019422

Printed in the USA

FOOD AND ENERGY

People love the smell of bacon cooking. People enjoy eating. But people don't live to eat. People eat to live. They need food for growth and energy. Energy gives people power to do things.

A green sea anemone begins to swallow a small sea star.

The same is true for ocean **organisms**. All of them must eat. As you might guess, big fish often eat little fish. That food link between bigger fish and smaller fish is easy to understand. But what did the little fish eat—an even smaller fish? Perhaps. What did that fish eat?

Food and its energy pass from one living thing to another. But it's not a very straight path. Let's take a closer look at how food and energy travel.

A tarpon rushes into a school of baitfish.

PLANKTON

Every meal of almost every **marine** animal begins with sunlight. How can that be?

Some of the smallest organisms in the ocean are plants. Many are too small to see without a **microscope**. But these tiny, floating plants are very important. They can turn sunlight into food! Even the tiniest organisms must eat.

These mini-plants are food for tiny, floating animals. Together, the floating plants and animals make up the ocean "stew" called **plankton**.

A hungry manta ray speeds into a cloud of plankton.

FOOD CHAINS

Plankton is dinner for all kinds of marine animals, including shrimp and their cousin, krill. Think of sunlight as the first link in a chain on which food travels. Plankton is the next link because plankton use sunlight.

Ocean plants turn sunlight into food.

A yellowtail surgeonfish grazes on plankton and bits of algae plants.

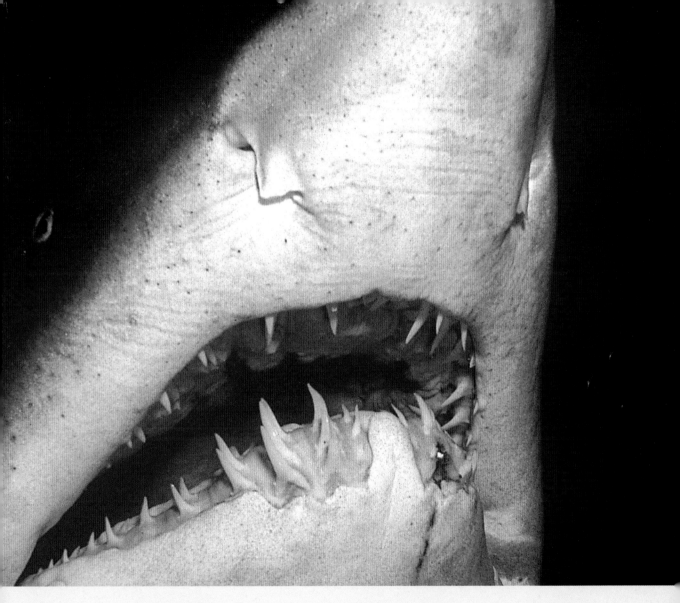

A sand tiger shark, one of the ocean's great predators, reveals toothy jaws.

The krill that eat plankton are the next link. If a seal eats the krill, it is also linked to the chain. Finally, a killer whale, or orca, becomes part of this food chain. The killer whale eats the seal. We can say sunlight is at the bottom of the chain. The killer whale is at the top.

Shrimp are an important prey for many kinds of sea animals.

A food chain like this helps show how food and energy move from one organism to another. But the path of food energy doesn't stop at the top of food chains. The killer whale will die. At least some of its remains will sink to the sea floor. There they will rot. Tiny organisms will feed on the dead whale. The whale disappears in time. But the food and energy stored in the whale's body doesn't. It travels from the whale to the living organisms that eat the whale's remains.

Wherever they live in the ocean, killer whales are at the top of food chains.

FOOD WEBS

Food chains are not simple. The killer whale, for example, doesn't just eat seals. And krill eat organisms other than plankton. If you linked all these marine animals, there would be many food chains. Drawn in pictures, the chains would look like a web.

The sea otter, here enjoying a clam, is near the top of many food chains.

A food web is made up of many chains that link. Most animals don't feed on just one kind of food. And they are not **prey** for just one kind of animal. Krill is a favorite food of some whales, penguins, and seabirds. That makes krill part of many food chains.

Each marine animal has a special place in food chains called a **niche**. Some animals eat plants. That is their niche. Some animals are **predators**. Predators eat other animals, their prey. Some animals eat plants and animals. Some animals are **scavengers**. Scavengers eat the remains of dead organisms.

Fish can hide and find food on coral reefs.

WONDERS OF MARINE LIFE

Ocean niches are filled with wonderful creatures. There are 14,000 kinds of marine fish. The smallest is less than one inch (2.5 centimeters) long. The largest is nearly 40 feet (12 meters) long.

And how about the great whales? The largest, the blue, can weigh 380,000 pounds (172,727 kilograms). That's the weight of 100 cars!

There are animals that look like plants, biscuits, bats, brains, and stars. There is a jellyfish 6 feet (2 m) wide and a squid more than 60 feet long (18 m).

GLOSSARY

marine (meh REEN) — of the sea

microscope (MY kreh skohp) — an instrument that helps people see things that are too small to see with just our eyes

niche (NICH) — the special place that a plant or animal fills in a living community of plants and animals

organism (OR gen IZ em) — a living, or once-living, thing

plankton (PLANGK ten) — the usually tiny, floating plants and animals of the seas

predator (PRED eh tor) — an animal that kills other animals for food

prey (PRAY) — an animal that is hunted by another animal for food

scavenger (SKAV in jer) — an animal that eats the remains of dead plants or animals

INDEX

Further Reading

Marquitty, Miranda. *Ocean*. Dorling Kindersley, 1995

World Book. *The Sea and Its Marvels*. World Book, 1997

Stone, L. *Fish*. Rourke Publishing, 1993

Websites To Visit

- www.abfla.com/parks/JohnPennekamp/pennekamp.html
- www.eco-pros.com/oceanhome.html

About The Author

Lynn Stone is the author of over 400 children's books. He is a talented natural history photographer as well. Lynn, a former teacher, travels worldwide to photograph wildlife in their natural habitat.